Decorating
with nature

Decorating
with nature

Janet Bridge

PUBLISHED BY
SALAMANDER BOOKS LIMITED
LONDON

A Salamander Book

Published by Salamander Books Ltd
8 Blenheim Court, Brewery Road,
London N7 9NT
United Kingdom

9 8 7 6 5 4 3 2 1

Editor: Joanna Smith
Art Editor: Mark Holt
Photographer: Simon Butcher
Photographer's Assistant: Giles Stokoe
Stylist: Janet Bridge
Original Design Concept: Town Group Consultancy
Colour Reproduction: Dah Hua Printing Press Co.,
Hong Kong
Printed and Bound in Slovenia

ACKNOWLEDGEMENTS
The author would like to thank Stephanie Symes at
Aria, Jason Waterworth at Nice Irma's and Louise
Green at RJ's Homeshop for their help in loaning
photographic props. Also, thanks to Raphael Cohen
at The Handmade Paper Company, David Hudson
at Ruckley Dried Flowers and John Owen at Craft
World for supplying materials. Special thanks to
Lyn Jones for her help in making the projects, to
Lisa Rackley and to my family for their continuous
support. Also, my sincere thanks to Simon Butcher
for his lovely photographs.

The publisher and author would like to thank the
following for their kind supply or loan of materials
and props:

Nice Irma's
46 Goodge Street
London W1P 1FJ
0171 580 6921
Plum chair (pages 42, 49, 50)
White muslin cushions (pages 90, 97)
Embroidered bed throw (page 90)

RJ's Homeshop
Furniture available from a large selection.
0171 681 9000 for stockist.
Savannah chest of drawers (pages 89, 92, 98)
Toulon table, lime (pages 58, 60, 62, 68)
Loire chair, lime (pages 60, 68)

Aria
133 Upper Street
Islington
London N1 1QP
0171 226 1021
Toothbrushes (page 112)
Waffle towel (page 107)
Bath brush (pages 108, 111)
Glass bottles (page 85)
Bedstead (pages 86, 90, 97)
Red suede notebook (page 85)
Leather-bound photo albums (page 85)
Glass bowls (page 38)

The Handmade Paper Co.
Acorn Business Centre
Wembley Stadium Industrial Estate
First Way
Wembley
Middlesex HA9 0HB
0181 903 6188

Ruckley Dried Flowers
Ruckley Estate Office
Shifnal
Shropshire TF11 8PQ
01952 460427

Craft World
Barnsdale Drive
Westcroft District Centre
Milton Keynes
Bucks. MK4 4DD
01908 520000

Bantock Flowers Ltd
Unit 8
Weldon Road
Loughborough
Leicestershire LE11 0RN
01509 232992

Silks Plant and Floral Services
52 Tenter Road
Moulton Park Industrial Estate
Nothants. NN3 6AX
01604 644488

Price's Patent Candle Co. Ltd
110 York Road
London SW11 3RU
0171 228 2001

Contents

Introduction

Decorating homes and work places with flowers and plants has been enjoyed by many for a very long time. Nothing brightens an otherwise dull corner or an empty table more than a colourful display of fresh flowers, and plants can be used to great effect to create an harmonious atmosphere in a room, especially if you are a follower of feng shui principles. However, have you ever thought of ways that other natural items can decorate and enhance the home? For instance, pressed flowers and leaves can be used in a variety of ways to decorate stationery, wrapped gifts, candles or lampshades. Shells and starfish can be used to decorate mirror frames, beakers, even curtain tie backs. Dried spices can be used to great effect in decorating due to their variety of shapes and colours and the same can be said for pulses. Think of the range of colours, from bright orange lentils to the shiny dark red of kidney beans or the shape and texture of star anise or cinnamon sticks. Dried flowers are widely used as an ever-lasting decoration around the home and in this book you will find ideas for using them in more unusual ways to create interesting, individual displays. Moss is also very versatile in decoration; you can use it to decorate the lids of boxes, terracotta pots and even create everlasting topiary shapes.

One of the advantages of using natural materials is that they are easily available, whether from the beach, woodland or even your own garden. Spices, pulses, fruits and vegetables are readily available from markets or supermarkets. There is an infinite number of ways that natural items can be used in decoration and I hope this book will enthuse and inspire you to create not only the projects included here, but encourage you to look upon natural materials in a new light.

Janet Bridge

Natural textures

Textures play an important role in home decoration and crafts. Natural materials vary greatly in this respect, so texture should be taken into consideration when selecting the items you intend to use to decorate your surroundings. To offer inspiration, below are examples of natural materials that fall into the following categories (clockwise from top left): hard, soft, rough and smooth.

Greens in nature

Of all the colours, green is the one that is most associated with nature. Green comes in a variety of shades, from the deep, rich green found in glossy ivy leaves to the palest green found in a spring cabbage. Its versatility is most apparent when looking at a cottage garden in summer. Green creates harmony in the riot of other colours and, at the same time, the various different greens found in the different plants actually add interest rather than conflict, which could be the case with other colours. Greens, particularly paler ones, create a feeling of peace and tranquillity when used in the home.

Yellows in nature

This colour scales the spectrum from the palest yellow of Saharan sand to the rich orange-yellows of exotic fruits such as kumquats. Bright yellow is the colour that represents the end of winter with the sight of aconites in woodland areas and drifts of yellow daffodils in grassy pastures. Yet it is also the colour of autumn, of harvests of golden wheat ripening on American plains and of sweetcorn ears in the late sunshine.

Browns and reds in nature

These are often referred to as earth colours and are sometimes regarded as dull and drab, a view which can easily be dismissed if one takes a closer look. For example, there is nothing more visually rich than piles of exotic spices, in shades of russet, gold and chestnut. Earth colours are, as the name implies, base colours that can be happily offset by many of the other colours in nature. Think of an old, weathered terracotta pot planted with bright summer flowers. Nothing suits the vivid mixture of flower colours more than the warm tones of the terracotta.

Whites in nature

White is generally considered to be pure and simple, but if you have ever visited a white-themed garden, you will know that there is a great diversity of whites. The tones and hues range from the purest white of the first snow-drop to the rich, creamy, heady white of garde-nia flowers. The variation can also be seen in the bright, hard white of smooth round peb-bles, the creamy white of garlic husks, rice and sesame seeds and the lovely soft tones of drift-wood that has been bleached by the sea. In interior design, it is a colour that reflects peace and a feeling of space.

Pinks in nature

Pinks are not necessarily colours directly associated with nature except, perhaps, as the colours of flowers such as sweet-smelling stocks, statuesque delphiniums and old-fashioned roses. However, pinks can be found in other natural materials such as pink peppercorns, rhubarb, potatoes and radishes and as pink patches on variegated leaves. Many shells have pale or dark pink tones, both inside and out, and pebbles, gravel and rocks often come in shades of dusky pink.

Drying and preserving

Fresh flower displays are, by their very nature, temporary and this is very much part of their charm. However, if a display is to last, or if you want to use flowers and leaves to decorate other items around the home, the material will have to be preserved to lengthen its life.

Air drying is the simplest method for drying flowers. All you need is a dry space such as an airing cupboard, loft or spare room with freely circulating air. Most flowers can be dried in bunches which should be hung from a pole suspended at least 30cm (1ft) from the ceiling. Make sure the bunches are not too close: they need to have air circulating around them. Some flowers, such as hydrangeas, can be dried individually to maintain their shape. Heavier, larger items such as artichokes and sweetcorn should be dried on a wire rack for best results. The stems are slotted through the mesh and the heads are supported in an upright position.

Air drying is the most commonly used method of preserving flowers. Choose a cool, airy room: if it is too warm, the flowers will dry too quickly and become brittle. Tie the flowers in bunches and hang from a pole, leaving space between the bunches for circulating air. Larger heads should be dried individually.

Heavy items, such as artichokes and sweetcorn, should be dried on a wire rack. Suspend a sheet of wire mesh tightly between two wooden blocks and insert the stems down through the holes in the mesh. For longer stems, suspend the mesh over a deep box or a space between two work surfaces.

Another method for drying flowers is with silica gel crystals. This method keeps the flowers looking fresher than traditional air drying. The flower heads are covered with the crystals which absorb moisture from the petals. It is important not to leave the flowers in the crystals for too long or they will become very brittle.

Pressed flowers and leaves are invaluable for decorating items in the home and it is simple to press them yourself. Collect the material on a dry day and lay carefully between two sheets of blotting paper or a double thickness of tissue. They can then be transferred to a flower press or placed between the pages of a heavy book. That's all there is to it.

Dried fruit slices also make great materials for decorating the home. Most fruits can be simply sliced and left to dry. Most are successful and it's worth experimenting with different fruits to see the effects that can be achieved.

There are three ways to dry fruit slices. The first is to lay them on a wire rack and leave in a warm, dark place until dry. The second is to place the rack in a very cool oven, with the door ajar. The last is to lay them on a plate and place in the microwave on defrost setting. Use short bursts of power to avoid scorching.

Traditional flower presses are available from craft shops, but a heavy book can have the same effect. Lay the flowers or leaves on blotting or tissue paper, making sure the petals are in the right position and none of the leaf edges is turned over. Cover with more paper and place in the press or in a heavy book.

When using silica gel to dry flowers, place some crystals in an air-tight container, place the flowers on top, then fill up the container with more crystals, easing them between the flower petals with a soft brush. Cover with the remaining crystals, put on the lid and leave for about two days until the flowers are dry.

Wiring cones and pods

Cones, seed pods and nuts can be used in many decorative ways around the home. In some instances, you may need to have a stem on the cone or pod to use it in a display, perhaps one where you are using the cones in a foam-based arrangement.

There are two ways to attach wires to cones, pods and nuts. One is with glue alone and the other is by inserting the wire into the item, but you may still need glue to hold it securely in place.

Where the seed pod is not too hard, the wire can be merely pushed through it, but if this is not possible, you will have to make a hole. This can be done with a thin, sharp tool such as a bradawl, or with a drill if the item in question is a nut or other very hard object. A small hand drill is best for the finest control, and choose as fine a drill bit as you can.

To form a stem for a cone, you will need heavy gauge stub wire available from florists or craft shops. Slip the wire between the scales of the cone, as near to the base of the cone as possible. You will be left with two wire ends. The shorter one should be about 5cm (2in) long.

Twist the two wire ends together, making sure the wire is wrapped tightly around the base of the cone. Bend the wires under the cone so that the stem appears to originate in the centre. If the wires will be at all visible in the display you are planning, cover them with brown crêpe tape.

Nuts are too smooth to twist a wire around and too hard to push a wire through, so the only option is to drill a hole through which to insert a wire. Use a drill with a very fine bit and drill the hole close to the base of the nut. You will probably have more control if you use a hand drill.

Push a heavy gauge stub wire into the hole in the nut and apply some strong, fast-drying glue around the hole to hold the wire in place. You will find that a glue gun is best suited to this task. The glue can be applied in a liberal coating which will dry very quickly and hold fast.

Seed pods which are relatively soft can have a wire pushed through close to the base. Again, leave one long end and one short end and twist the ends together to hold the wire in place. If it is not possible to simply push the wire through, make a hole with a bradawl or a drill with a fine bit.

With some seed pods, especially those with a flat side, it is easier to simply glue the wire to the outside. To do this, make a small loop at one end of the wire and place it against the flat side of the pod. Smother the wire loop with strong, fast-drying glue and hold in place until set.

Wiring flowers and fruit

The addition of wire to a flower or leaf stem can add extra support when making swags or other arrangements with either fresh or dried materials. Most flowers and leaves, whether fresh or preserved, will already have a perfectly good stem, but if you have a bent or damaged stem or you need a much longer stem for the arrangement you are planning, wires are the answer.

To wire a flower or leaf stem, you will need two different sorts of wire: fine rose wire and heavy gauge stub wire. Both are available from florists and craft suppliers. The rose wire is used to bind the existing flower or leaf stem to the stub wire which acts as the new stem.

If you suspect that the wire stem will be visible in the arrangement, you may want to cover it with crêpe tape or gutta percha tape which will help to make the wire look like a natural green or brown stem. Crêpe tape is

To wire a leaf or flower, first cut off the flower head or leaf leaving about 2.5cm (1in) of stem. Hold the stem and a stub wire together and add a rose wire to the bundle, leaving a long end at the top. Wind the top end of the rose wire back down the bundle, binding all three elements tightly together.

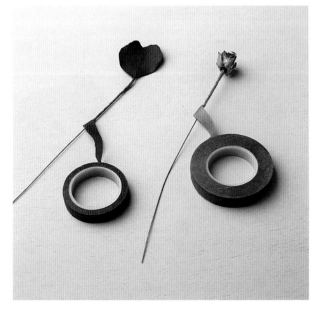

To cover a wire stem with crêpe tape or gutta percha, roll the neck of the flower or leaf over the end of the tape which is held at 45° to the wire stem. Twist the wire repeatedly to wrap the tape round and round the wire, all the time working down the stem. Keep the tape taut at all times.

ribbed and slightly sticky, whereas gutta percha is smooth and more waterproof, making it suitable for both fresh and dried arrangements. Both are self-adhesive, but must be kept in an airtight tin to remain in good condition.

Almost anything can be used in a display if it adds a decorative quality and many of the more unusual elements will need to have wires attached to secure them in the arrangement. For example, many fresh fruits are very attractive indeed and add bright colours and a pleasant aroma to table centrepieces. These can be wired using just a single stub wire which is pushed right through the base of the fruit. The two ends are then twisted together to hold the wire in place.

Small terracotta pots are also very attractive when used in displays such as the kitchen collage on page 29. These are wired in a slightly different way which is described below.

Most fruits and vegetables can be wired, as long as the flesh is strong enough that the wire does not just tear through it. Pass the end of a stub wire through the fruit close to the base, leaving one of the wire ends short and the other long. Twist the ends together to hold the wire in place.

To wire a terracotta flower pot, first make a double loop at one end of a long, heavy gauge stub wire and wrap the short end round and round the middle of the double loop to hold it firm. Pass the other end of the wire through the hole in the pot and pull it through so the loop sits on the base of the pot inside.

Flatten the loops against the bottom of the pot and smother them with strong, fast-drying glue. A glue gun will have best results. Hold the wire in position until the glue is dry. If the inside of the flower pot will be visible in the display, you can disguise the wire with a small piece of moss glued over it.

THE KITCHEN

Raffia storage jars

Use this idea to transform a range of odd storage jars, pots and bottles into a colourful, matching set to complement the kitchen. Raffia is available in both its natural colour and dyed in a selection of bright shades. Being a natural product, it is rather variable, so carefully select a number of long, even pieces and trim off the ragged ends before you begin to cover the jars.

1. Paint a line of glue around the neck of the jar and several others running vertically down the sides. Start by winding a length of raffia around the neck of the jar over the line of glue, untwisting it as you go. Continue working down around the jar.

2. When you come to the end of the length of raffia, glue it firmly to the jar, and glue the start of the next piece over the top. When the jar is covered, leave to dry. Then tie pieces of coloured raffia around the jar in rings and trim the ends.

Materials & Tools

storage jars

plain and coloured raffia

scissors

glue

glue brush

darning needle

3. To make the zig-zag pattern, thread some raffia onto a large needle. Slip it under one of the pieces of raffia covering the jar and tie in place. Bring it across to the next point and tie again; continue around the jar. Finish by interspersing with small knots.

Fruit and vegetable collage

This is one of those projects where your imagination can run wild. Collages, by definition, are a collection of different items which could range from dried and artificial fruits and vegetables, to wooden utensils, dried flowers or even garden implements. You could add some fresh items and replace when necessary. For instance, fresh apples and sweetcorn could be used with dried wheat bunches for a harvest arrangement.

1. Cover the foam with a double layer of nylon, tie the ends and cut off excess. Push both ends of a long wire through the foam to the back, twist the ends and make a loop for hanging. Cover the foam with straw held in place with wire staples.

2. Attach wires to the terracotta pots and dried and artificial materials using the wiring techniques explained on pages 22 and 23. Tie three dried or artificial garlic heads together with raffia and wire together loops of decorative cord.

Materials & Tools

dry oasis foam

nylon sock or stocking

straw or fine wood shavings

small terracotta pots

heavy gauge wire

glue gun, scissors

decorative cord or string

raffia

dried grasses and wheat

dried fruits, vegetables, spices

artificial vegetables

3. Assemble the collage starting from the base, overlapping the materials to hide the straw. Insert the wires into the foam, right through to the back, to hold the items securely in place. Arrange the materials carefully to achieve a bold but balanced effect.

Fruit and spice mobiles

Many different dried fruits and spices can be threaded together to make interesting kitchen mobiles. Cinnamon sticks, dried chillies, nutmegs and bay leaves are especially good, as are many different whole or sliced fruits. Drying your own fruit slices is not difficult and much cheaper than buying them (see page 19). Try to wear protective gloves when handling chillies and work in a well-ventilated room.

1. Take two long pieces of string and knot together at one end. Tie a small twig to the strings just above the knot then thread both the loose ends through the eye of the darning needle.

2. Choose three orange slices of a similar size and thread them onto the string above the twigs. Next add four slices of dried kiwi fruit, then four slices of dried star fruit.

Materials & Tools

rough string

darning needle

small twigs

dried fruit slices

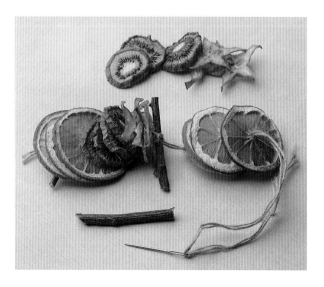

3. Tie a knot in the string just above the star fruit slices, then tie another short twig in position above this. Repeat with further slices of fruit and twigs until you have achieved the required length. Try a few variations using other fruits or spices.

Herb basket

The attraction of this basket is not just its appearance but also the aromatic scent from the dried herbs. Herbs are very easy to dry and tend to retain their fragrance. They can be simply hung in an airy room to dry (for more details, see page 18). The basket could be used to store foods such as eggs or garlic bulbs, but it could also be filled with an arrangement of more dried herbs and be purely decorative.

1. Use lengths of reel wire to sew the moss onto the front of the basket, working the wire ends between the basket weave and twisting the ends together at the back. Leave the edges of the moss sheets ragged to add to the final appearance.

Materials & Tools

wall basket

dried sheet moss

reel wire

dried herbs such as oregano, sage and peppermint

raffia

2. Gather the herb stems into small bunches and secure with wire. Attach the bunches to the basket with wire, starting in the centre and working out both sides, with the heads overlapping the stems of the previous bunch. Make the sides symmetrical.

3. Take another bunch of herbs and tie raffia around the stems to cover the wire. Thread a longer length of raffia through the edge of the basket and tie the bunch in place to cover the bare stems of the last bunch on the basket. Repeat on the other side.

Rose display box

Display frames are ever popular and a great way of using natural materials to create a picture within a frame. They can be purchased empty from craft shops or florist suppliers. The materials should be chosen for their colours and textures, especially if you are making the frame for a specific place. Make sure that the smaller items are glued in place or you may find them appearing in other compartments.

1. Glue pieces of ribbon to the box edges to decorate. Glue slices of dried kiwi into the central section, add an orange slice next and top with a star anise. Glue the rose heads into the four outer sections, arranging them as closely together as possible.

2. When the roses are securely fixed, glue small pieces of sheet moss over the top of the yellow ribbon, allowing the colour to show through. Next, mix the fennel seeds with thinned glue until well coated and spoon into the empty sections. Leave to dry.

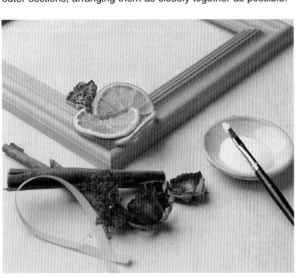

3. Finally, decorate one corner of the outer frame using dried fruit slices, rose heads and the cinnamon sticks. Finish with a little more dried moss and a piece of ribbon. Assemble the frame when the glue is dry, first checking everything is secure.

Materials & Tools

empty display box

dried rose heads

fennel seeds

dried kiwi and orange slices

star anise

cinnamon sticks

PVA glue (white household glue)

glue brush

thin ribbon

dried sheet moss

Oil and vinegar bottles

Sprigs of fresh or dried herbs can transform an ordinary bottle into something more unusual. The herbs tied onto the neck of the bottle could reflect the flavour of the oil or vinegar inside, or you could simply choose them for their decorative qualities, adding dried spices or chillies for added interest. These bottles would make an attractive gift, particularly at Christmas time. Remember to wear gloves for handling chillies.

1. Cover the top of the bottle with a square of brown paper (or fabric if you prefer) and hold in place with an elastic band. Select two or three sprigs of a herb such as rosemary and cut a long length of thick twine.

2. Tie the twine around the herb stems leaving the twine ends about equal lengths. Next thread three or four bay leaves onto a short piece of fine twine using the darning needle. Knot both ends and tie onto the thick twine next to the herb sprigs.

Materials & Tools

brown paper or fabric

thick twine

fine twine

fresh herbs such as rosemary

dried or fresh bay leaves

darning needle

scissors

elastic band

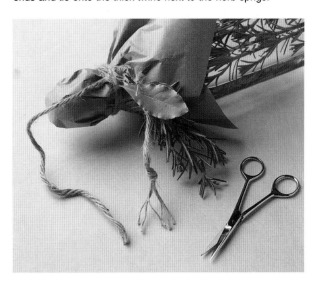

3. Tie the two ends of the twine together in a knot just above the herbs, then wrap the twine around the neck of the bottle several times and finish in a secure knot. Tie a knot in both ends of the twine and trim off the excess.

THE SITTING ROOM

Topiary tree

Materials & Tools

12.5cm (5in) terracotta pot

12.5cm (5in) dry oasis ball

10cm (4in) topiary base

30cm (12in) cane

dried wheat, elastic bands

sheet moss, glue, wire staples

decorative string, scissors

Wheat has been used for decoration for many years, often to make corn dollies or harvest arrangements. This topiary tree uses wheat in a very different way to create a precise, structured arrangement where the uniformity of the wheat has been exploited to the full. This tree will make an eye-catching feature on its own, but you could also make two and display one on either side of a table, doorway or fireplace.

1. Glue moss around the terracotta pot to cover it completely and allow to dry. Cut the wheat ears from the stems, leaving about 2.5cm (1in) of stem on each ear.

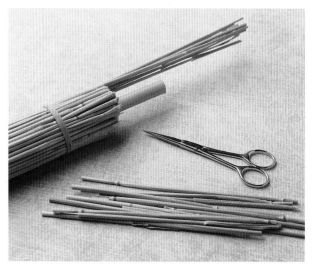

2. Bunch up the discarded wheat stems and hold the bundle together with an elastic band at each end. Insert the cane through the centre of the bundle, then trim the stems down to leave 5cm (2in) of bare cane at either end.

3. Push one end of the cane into the topiary base and the other into the foam ball, and glue. Glue the topiary base into the flower pot. Secure one end of the string onto the bottom of the ball with a wire staple and glue. Start to arrange the wheat ears.

4. When the wheat ears are arranged evenly in the ball and all the gaps have been filled, wrap and glue the string down and around the trunk in a spiral fashion. Continue the string in a spiral over the surface of the pot to cover the topiary base.

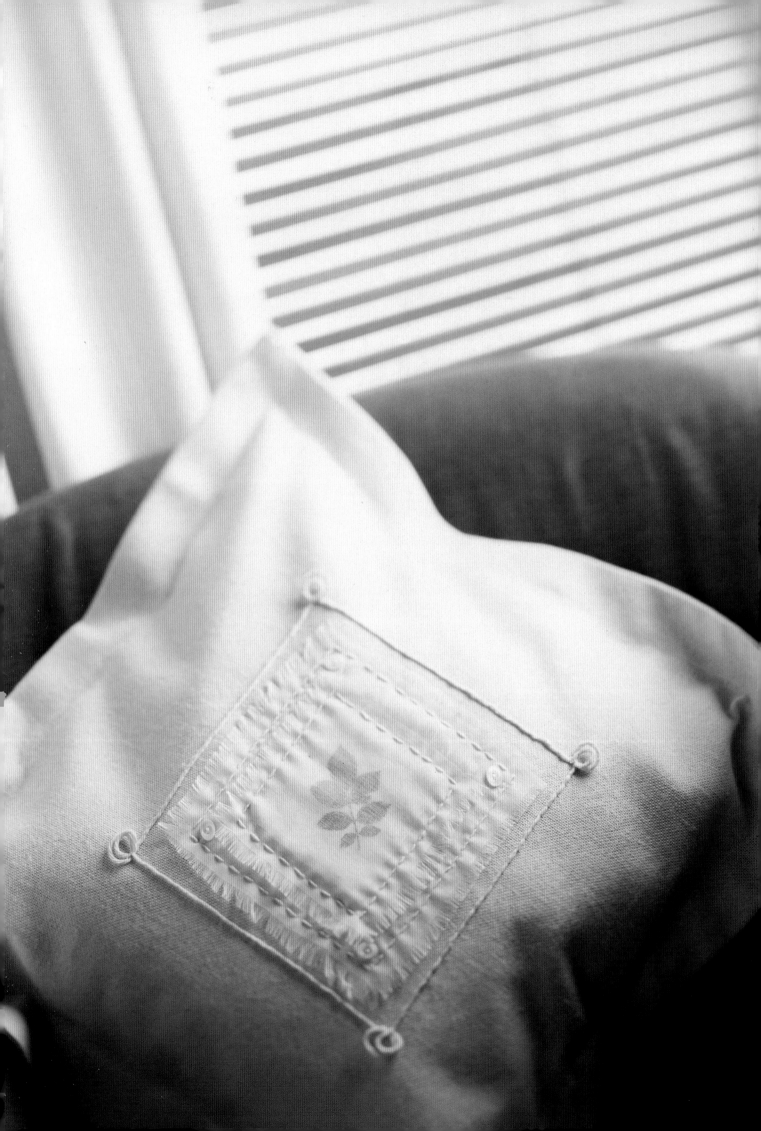

Pressed leaf cushion

This attractive cushion could be displayed in a sitting room or bedroom: its neutral tones will complement most colour schemes. If you want to add more colour to it, or even make a selection of different cushions, you could use pressed flowers or coloured leaves instead. Choose leaves or flowers that are not too brittle otherwise they will crumble. A coat of varnish on the leaves will help to strengthen them.

Materials & Tools

cream cushion cover and pad

pressed rose leaves

muslin, cream cotton fabric

flexible glue and brush

thick cotton thread

needle, cotton, scissors, pins

4 neutral buttons

1. Cut two squares of muslin, one 15cm (6in) and one 12.5cm (5in) across. Cut one square of cream fabric 8cm (3¹/₄in) across. Fray the edges on all sides of the three squares by removing the outer threads to a depth of about 1cm (¹/₂in).

2. Stick the cotton square onto the large muslin square using the flexible glue. Next glue the pressed rose leaf in the centre of the cotton square and allow the glue to dry. Lay the smaller muslin square on top.

3. Pin the squares onto the centre of the cushion cover, making sure they lie flat. Sew the squares to the cushion cover using the thick cotton thread to make large tacking stitches. Sew a line of stitches around the edge of each of the muslin squares.

4. Use the needle and cotton to sew a button to each corner of the outer muslin square. Lastly pin, then sew, a length of thick cotton thread around the outside of the muslin to form a line of decorative piping with a double loop at each corner.

Tiered display

This style of arrangement is becoming very popular as a more sculptured and stylish alternative to the traditional presentation of dried flowers. It is not difficult to achieve as long as each layer is clearly defined. You could create many alternatives in this style. A similar display using wheat stems of different lengths tied round with raffia, for example, could look very attractive in a kitchen setting.

1. Cut the dry florist's foam down to size using a carving knife, making sure it fits tightly into the terracotta pot. The edges of the foam should be level with the rim of the pot. Pin a layer of moss around the outer edge of the foam using wire staples.

2. Start with some daisies in the centre, pushing the stems into the foam until the tops are level. Next add a ring of larkspur around the daisies, again with the tops level, but this time lower. Continue with rings of material, each lower than the last.

3. When the bare foam is covered, right to the edges of the moss, finish with a single line of wheat ears arranged as neatly as possible. Check all the layers of material are level and add extra moss if any bare foam is visible.

Materials & Tools

dried larkspur

dried wheat

dried michaelmas daisies

long cinnamon sticks

dry florist's foam

terracotta pot

dried sheet moss

wire staples

scissors

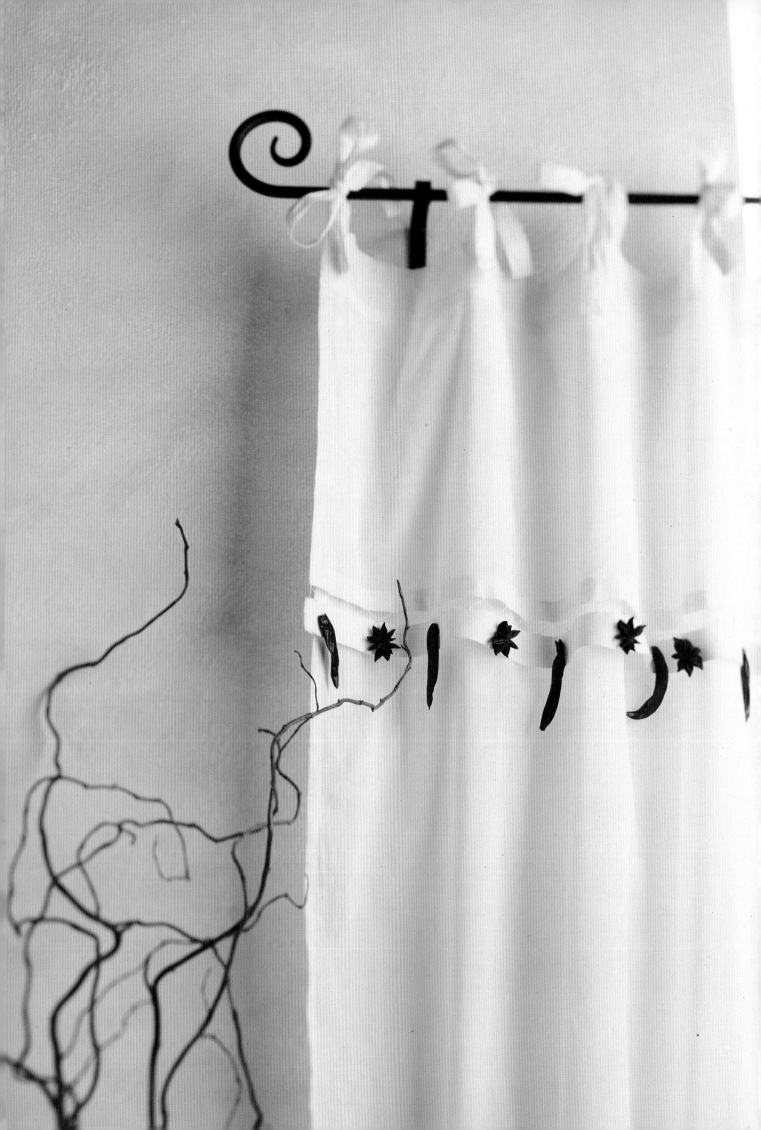

Sheer curtains

Using spices to decorate curtains is a rather unusual but interesting idea. Here we have used star anise, with its attractive shape and appealing aniseed scent, and dried chillies for their rich colour. The spices are attached to a tape which is sewn in a loose herringbone stitch to the curtain pelmet. Be careful when handling chillies: avoid contact with the eyes and work in a well-ventilated room.

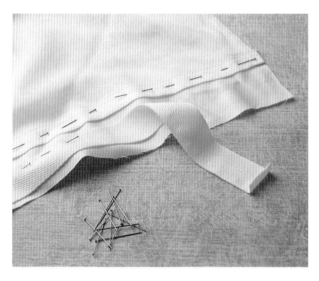

1. Pin the bottom edge of the curtain pelmet to a strip of scrap fabric making sure it lies flat. Next, pin the cotton tape to the fabric, leaving an even gap of about 1cm (1/2in) between the tape and the edge of the pelmet.

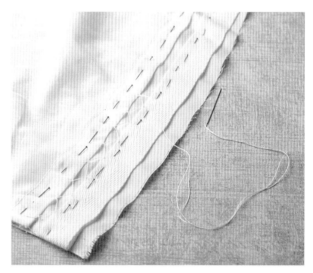

2. Use the crochet thread to sew herringbone stitches between the pelmet and the tape, making a double stitch occasionally for added strength. Remember not to pass the needle through the scrap fabric. Remove the pins and the fabric and press.

Materials & Tools

sheer curtain with pelmet

2.5cm (1in) deep cotton tape

white crochet thread

long strip of scrap fabric

star anise

dried chillies

needle

scissors

dressmaking pins

glue and brush

3. Glue the star anise and the chillies to the tape spacing them evenly along its length. Allow the glue to dry. When the curtains need to be washed, remove the tape by cutting through the stitches and sew back in place in the same way after washing.

Curtain tie back

Materials & Tools

90cm (36in) of 5cm (2in) hessian

3.6m (12ft) of wide piping cord

rivet gun and rivets

glue gun or strong glue

needle and brown cotton

string or cord, shells

scissors, dressmaking pins

All of the materials needed for this tie back are available from craft suppliers, but you may prefer to use shells that you have collected yourself so the tie back becomes a fond reminder of a past vacation. A glue gun is a definite advantage when making this as the glue dries very quickly. This allows you to keep holding the tie back against the curtain as you go to check the design and achieve the best results.

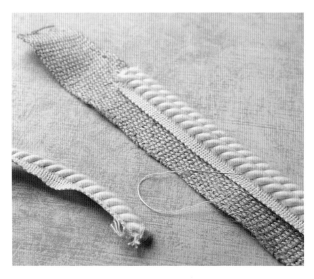

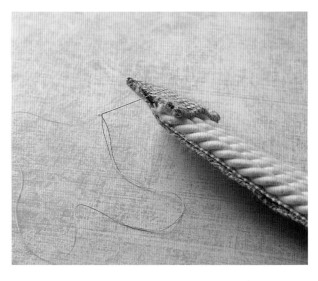

1. Cut the piping into five equal lengths. Sew the first piece to one edge of the hessian, leaving an equal length of bare hessian at either end. Sew on the next three pieces in the same way. Remove the braiding from the last piece and glue in place.

2. Fold the end of the hessian over to cover the ends of the piping, tuck under the raw edge and pin. Sew neatly around the edges of the hessian and across the piping, ensuring that all the raw edges have been covered. Repeat with the other end.

3. Use the rivet gun to insert a rivet through the hessian at either end of the tie back. Thread a short length of string or cord through the rivet and tie the ends together to make a loop. The two loops will hold the tie back onto a hook in the wall.

4. Finally add the shells using a glue gun or strong glue to fix them in place. You could stick a selection of shells to the middle of the tie back or arrange them evenly along its length, depending on the effect you wish to achieve.

Dried hydrangeas

This simple, stunning arrangement owes part of its charm to the fact that it contains just one type of flower, interspersed with fine twigs. It is easy to dry hydrangeas yourself at home as long as they are picked when at their best during a dry spell. They should be hung upside down in a dry place (see page 18 for further details). You could use any other type of dried flower but hydrangeas do make a nice rounded mass.

1. Cut the foam block so it fits loosely into the vase with space around it on all sides. Place a handful of moss into the bottom of the vase and place the foam block on top. Push moss around the sides of the foam until the vase is full and the foam hidden.

2. Spread a layer of glue on the top surface of the foam block and push the foam ball onto it. Insert a strong stub wire through the top of the foam ball and push it right through into the foam block. This will hold the ball in position.

Materials & Tools

dried hydrangea heads

glass vase

dry foam block

dry foam ball

knife

green reindeer moss

florist's stub wire

preserved tree ivy

twigs

strong glue

3. Cut the ivy into small sprigs and insert them in a ring around the base of the foam ball. Next arrange the hydrangea heads in the foam to form a dense, even mass, checking the overall shape from time to time. Insert the twigs amongst the flowers.

Wall swag

A ready-made swag base will make this project quick and simple to achieve. Swag bases are readily available from florist or craft suppliers and come in a range of sizes: select one to suit its intended position. There are so many dried flowers, grasses and exotics available now that you could create any style or colour of swag you like. Swags look most effective when displayed over a mirror, doorway or a window.

1. Arrange the flowers, grasses and the smaller seedpods into small bunches and bind the stems together with reel wire. Cut the stems down if necessary. The larger seedpods and cones can be attached to the swag separately.

2. Starting at one end, pin the bunches to the swag with the stems facing the centre of the swag. Overlap the bunches so that the heads of one cover the stems of the last. Attach bunches using wire staples, but use glue for the individual pods.

Materials & Tools

swag base

dried flowers and grasses

assorted seedpods and cones

reel wire

wire staples

glue gun

3. When you reach the centre of the swag, start again from the other end aiming for an even balance, again pointing the stems towards the centre. Finish the swag by gluing a selection of pods and cones over the remaining bare stems in the centre.

THE DINING ROOM

Ivy napkins and centrepiece

Materials & Tools

long ivy trails

tree ivy branches

bowl, wet florist's foam, tape

green chrysanthemums

white lilies, pink stocks

white september flower

reel wire, pruning shears

Ivy lends itself well to flower arranging as the long stems can be used to create a framework to shape the arrangement. In this centrepiece the ivy stems have been used to form the oval outline, a shape which is ideal for a rectangular table. If you have a round table, cut all the stems to the same length and make a circular display. The lilies add a formal note but could be omitted for a more relaxed occasion.

1. Soak the foam, then secure in the bowl using florist's tape. Insert a ring of large ivy leaves into the sides of the foam to cover the bowl. Insert some long trails at the sides of the display and shorter ones at the front and back to make an oval outline.

2. Tuck some chrysanthemum heads amongst the ivy and add long and short lengths of September flower to accentuate the oval shape of the display. Add pieces of tree ivy and white lilies to add height, all the time working within the oval outline.

3. Continue to add the white and green materials, aiming to achieve a balance of colour and a domed, oval shape. Intersperse with the pink stocks, distributing them evenly through the display. Check all sides to make sure there are no gaps.

4. To make the napkin rings, wind some young, flexible ivy trails into a circle and hold them together with reel wire. Trim some small leaves from another piece of ivy and tuck the stems under the wire on the napkin ring to try to disguise it.

Fragrant posies

Fresh flowers create a pretty and inviting setting for dinner guests, especially if you decorate each place setting with its own little display. These fragrant posies are perfect for the dinner table. They are not too tall so won't prevent guests seeing each other and their fragrance will add to their appeal.

1. Start to make the posy by holding one stem in your hand and adding other stems around it in a criss-cross fashion. Continue to add stems of flowers and foliage until you have a rounded, even posy shape. Make sure you use lots of foliage.

Materials & Tools

fragrant flowers such as pinks,

freesias and cornflowers

foliage

string

pruning shears or strong scissors

washed gravel

sundae dish or small vase

2. Finish by adding a ring of foliage around the outside of the posy, then tie the stems tightly together with string at the point at which they all cross. Trim the stems level at the bottom so the posy will stand upright in the sundae dish.

3. Hold the posy in the dish with the stems in the centre and fill in the space around the stems with washed gravel. Fill the sundae dish with water and top up as necessary.

Cornflower candle pot

This is an unusual way of presenting flowers. Although it looks quite complicated, it is in fact simply made from a terracotta pot, a moss-covered ring, some fresh flowers and a large candle. The moss ring sits on the rim of the terracotta pot and the fresh flowers and candle are displayed within it. When the flowers fade, they can be simply removed and replaced by fresh ones.

1. Line the terracotta pot with plastic, trimming the edges just below the pot rim. Stand the candle in the pot and tightly pack pieces of foam around it to fill the pot. Pour water over the foam and leave to soak. Top up again until the foam is saturated.

2. Attach the reel wire to the wire ring. Take a handful of moss and lay over the ring, then wind the wire around it and the ring to hold it in place. Work your way around the ring, adding more moss and winding the wire tightly round until the ring is covered.

3. Lay the moss ring on top of the pot rim, then fill the space between the ring and the candle with fresh flowers, trimming down the stems and inserting them into the moist foam. Aim for an even balance of flowers and foliage of different colours.

Materials & Tools

large candle

thick plastic sheeting

wet florist's foam

terracotta pot

wire ring wreath base

preserved reindeer moss

reel wire

scissors, knife

blue cornflowers

green chrysanthemums

fresh foliage

Willow candle holders

You will need fresh willow wands, which are long and flexible, to make these candle holders. It is best to cut them before they come into leaf in spring, but if they do have leaves, remove them close to the stem and cut off the woody stem ends before use. The willow wands are woven into rings and three or four of the rings are stacked on top of a moss-covered ring and decorated with either seeds and nuts or with shells.

Materials & Tools

small polystyrene ring

green sheet moss

fresh willow wands

small cones, seeds and beans

glue and glue brush

scissors, florist's stub wires

candle in small glass holder

1. Paint patches of glue onto the polystyrene ring and stick on pieces of sheet moss. Continue until the ring is covered all over, then trim off any straggly ends of moss.

2. To make the willow rings, take a long wand and wind it round two or three times into a tight circle. Wrap the remaining thin end round and round the other strands to hold the circle in place. Make three or four rings for each candle holder.

3. Bend short lengths of wire into staples and use them to attach the willow rings to the moss-covered ring, one at a time. If the wire staples are very visible, glue small pieces of moss on top to cover them.

4. Finish the candle holder by gluing small cones, dried beans and seeds around the outsides of the willow rings. Place the candle in its little glass holder in the centre.

Celebration swags

Fresh flower swags can look very impressive and are particularly suited to special occasions such as weddings. The flowers and foliage are first made into small bunches and these bunches are then used to make the swags. They are wired to a backing, such as a piece of rope, with the flower heads of each bunch covering the stems of the last one. You will need a lot of flowers for a swag but it is well worthwhile.

1. Prepare the flower and foliage stems by cutting them into short lengths. Cut the rope to the length you want the swag to be, then make a loop at one end and wire in place. Leave the wire attached to the rope.

2. Arrange the flowers and foliage into small bunches. Hold the first bunch against the rope, covering the loop with the flowers, and bind the stems tightly to the rope using the wire. Add the next bunch in the same way, overlapping the stems of the first.

Materials & Tools

rope

strong scissors or pruning shears

reel wire

white viburnum

green chrysanthemums

red roses

white september flower

green and purple foliage

3. Continue binding bunches to the rope right along its length, making sure none of the stems shows. When you come to the end of the rope, make another loop and secure tightly with the wire. Cover the final stems with a ribbon or another swag.

Ice vase

An ice bowl makes an impressive centrepiece and could be used in a variety of ways: to serve a salad or a dessert, or as a vase if you make a tall, thin one. Follow the instructions below, then when you remove it from the freezer, plunge into cold water until the outer glass vessel comes free; leave the inner one in place if you are arranging flowers in it and display the vase in a bowl to catch the drips.

1. Crush the ice with a hammer. Place a layer of crushed ice in the large vessel and place the smaller one inside on top of the ice. Snip the heads off the flowers and cut the foliage into sprigs.

2. Drop some flowers and foliage into the space between the two containers, then add more crushed ice. Gradually work your way up the vase adding flowers, foliage and crushed ice until you reach the top of the vessels.

Materials & Tools

1 large glass vessel

1 small glass vessel

ice

hammer

chilled, boiled water

fresh flowers and foliage

scissors

heavy weight

3. Place something heavy in the inner vessel; we used plastic bags filled with pulses. Carefully pour the chilled, boiled water over the ice between the vessels until it reaches the top. Place in a freezer in an upright position overnight.

Flower and herb napkins

Fresh herbs have a delightful fragrance and make an appealing addition tucked inside a napkin as an informal decoration. Here we have added a single rose for colour, but you could replace this with herb flowers, such as chives, for a pretty, country style. Herbs with soft, green foliage will be most effective, like marjoram, oregano, soft thyme, tarragon, dill, coriander or fennel.

1. Cut the herb stems to length and gather into a loose bundle, mixing the different varieties evenly through the bunch. Add a single flower, then bind the bunch together with rose wire.

2. Cover the stems with gutta percha or crêpe tape. Start winding it around the stems at their tops and continue down to the ends of the stems, winding it tightly. Cut off the excess.

3. Iron and then fold the napkin and tie it loosely round with a ribbon. Slip the flower and herb posy under the ribbon.

Materials & Tools

fresh herb foliage

1 rose

rose wire

gutta percha or crêpe tape

ribbon

napkin

scissors

THE STUDY

Fruit stamped stationery

When used for printing, cut fruits can produce interesting shapes, such as the broken spots made by kumquats or the stars made by star fruits. Citrus fruits, such as lemons and oranges, are particularly effective, as the segments show up in the prints. Here we have used fruits to print motifs on writing paper and matching envelopes. It is important to blot the cut face of the fruit on absorbent paper before printing.

1. Cut the ends off the kumquats and blot on absorbent paper. Paint the face of the large kumquat with copper paint and stamp in the middle of the paper at the top. Repeat with a small kumquat, stamping on both sides of the large motif.

2. Paint the remaining small kumquat with the red paint and stamp a red motif over each of the copper ones, leaving a copper border around the red on the large motif. Don't worry if the copper paint is still wet as it will enhance the effect.

Materials & Tools

1 large and 2 small kumquats

writing paper and envelopes

copper acrylic paint

dark red acrylic paint

paint brush

knife

absorbent paper

3. Finish by stamping another copper motif over the top of the red ones to make a total of three layers of paint. This will produce a rich, deep colour. Print the envelopes in the same way, perhaps with just one motif in the middle of each flap.

Handmade cards

Making your own greetings cards is very quick and easy. Blank cards can be purchased from craft shops, but it is simple to make your own from thick paper. Handmade paper will enhance the organic style of the card and is available in a variety of textures and colours. The design can be adapted to include any natural material as long as it is not too bulky to fit in the envelope.

1. Cut a piece of corrugated card to fit the centre of the greetings card, leaving a margin of about 2.5cm (1in) of plain card around all sides. Stick the corrugated card in place using PVA glue (white household glue).

2. Next make an irregular rectangle of handmade paper. To do this, wet along the line you wish to tear with water and a small paintbrush, using a ruler as a guide. Tear along the wet line to leave an attractive ragged edge. Stick the paper to the card.

Materials & Tools

blank greetings cards

corrugated paper

handmade paper

star anise

dried chillies

scissors

PVA glue (white household glue)

glue brush

ruler

fine paintbrush and water

3. Finally, place the chillies and the star anise in position on the card. When you are happy with the arrangement, glue them carefully in place and when the glue is dry, check that they are attached firmly to the card.

75

Wrapped gifts

You can make an ordinary wrapped gift much more decorative simply by adding a pressed flower to it. Pressing flowers is very easy to do and the technique is explained on page 19. Make sure the flower is glued firmly to the parcel: loose petals will be easily damaged, though the cellophane will offer protection. Pressed leaves offer a pleasant, and perhaps more masculine-looking, alternative to pressed flowers.

1. Wrap the gift in the usual way using handmade or plain wrapping paper. Position the flowers on the gift and use the glue to stick them in place.

2. Cut a strip of coloured cellophane, narrower than the gift but long enough to wrap all the way round it. Use sticky tape to hold it in place at the back.

3. Tie two lengths of thin ribbon or raffia around the gift, one covering each edge of the cellophane strip. Secure the ribbon or raffia in place with a small neat knot and trim the ends.

Materials & Tools

plain wrapping paper

pressed flowers

coloured cellophane

PVA glue (white household glue)

glue brush

sticky tape

thin ribbon or raffia

scissors

Terracotta storage pots

Ordinary flower pots can be used successfully as storage pots; small sizes could be used to store pencils and pens, while larger ones could house rolls of paper or other bulky items. The use of terracotta in the home is very pleasing to the eye and it lends itself well to simple decoration. Ferns have a particularly interesting shape which needs no further enhancement, except perhaps some natural twine as used here.

1. Cut the fern to size so that it fits neatly onto the side of the pot. Paint the underside with thinned PVA glue (white household glue) using the paint brush. Do not thin the glue too much or the fern will peel away from the pot before the glue dries.

2. Press the fern piece firmly onto the side of the pot, ensuring it lies flat on the surface, and allow glue to dry. Once dry, give the fern and surrounding pot a coat of thinned PVA glue (white household glue) to protect the leaves from wear. Allow to dry.

Materials & Tools

terracotta pot

pressed fern

PVA glue (white household glue)

glue brush

scissors

natural twine

3. Wind the twine three times around the rim of the pot, using glue to hold the strands in position. Tie the strands together at intervals around the pot using more twine. Knot neatly and trim the ends short.

Decorated notebooks

Plain notebooks of all sizes, and folders too, can be decorated with pressed leaves. Here the notebooks chosen were made from handmade paper which suits this style of decoration well. There are many leaves of varying shapes and colours that press well. Pressing is not difficult: make sure the leaves are lying flat and press in the same way as flowers. See page 19 for further details of the technique.

1. Position the pieces of fern or other leaves on the front of the notebook, bearing in mind the width of the ribbon. Paint the undersides of the leaves with glue and press them in place.

2. Once the glue has dried, thin a little more glue with some water and use to paint the surface of the leaves. Thinned PVA glue (white household glue) acts like varnish and will protect the leaves.

Materials & Tools

notebook

pressed leaves

PVA glue (white household glue)

glue brush

scissors

ribbon

double-sided sticky tape

3. Position the strip of ribbon to cover the ends of the pieces of fern or leaves. Fold the ends of the ribbon over and stick firmly to the inside of the book cover using double-sided sticky tape.

Seeded picture frame

Seeds and pulses are very versatile and can be used in a variety of ways as decoration. They are not only interesting in colour, but can create different textures too. For example, the sesame seeds make a textural border around the smooth black beans and contrast sharply with them. When applying small seeds, it is wise to work over a tray or wide dish in which to catch the excess seeds. These can then be used again.

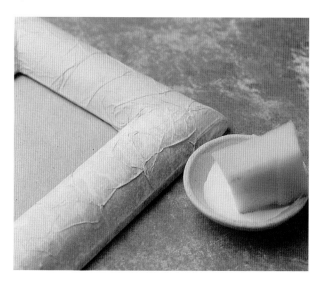

1. Paint the frame with the acrylic paint and leave to dry. Next sponge on the glaze to give a blotched effect. Before the glaze dries, gently brush the surface with a clean, dry sponge to soften the effect and give a more natural appearance.

2. Once the glaze is thoroughly dry, paint a line of glue around the inner edge of the frame. Stick the black beans to the glue, one at a time, aligning them all at the same angle. Position them tightly together to create a solid border. Allow to dry.

Materials & Tools

wood or papier mâché frame

stone-coloured vinyl silk paint

cream-coloured acrylic glaze

sponge

paintbrush

black beans

sesame seeds

strong glue

glue brush

varnish

3. Now paint a wider border of glue around the outside of the line of black beans. Sprinkle sesame seeds thickly over the glue and press them in place with your fingers. Shake off the excess and allow the glue to dry. Finish with a coat of varnish.

83

Storage boxes

Small papier mâché boxes can be enhanced simply but effectively using reindeer moss with other natural items. Reindeer moss is very versatile and as it is preserved, it won't dry out and become brittle. Once the moss has been glued to the lid, other items can be added such as the small bundle of twigs shown here. You could also add cinnamon sticks or other spices for their rich scents.

1. Tear the reindeer moss into pieces and glue them securely to the lid of the box, aiming for an even coverage.

2. Break some of the twigs into short lengths and tie about three pieces into a bundle using raffia. Glue to the lid of the box.

3. Split the ends of the raffia into fine, decorative strands, then glue one or two small cones on top of the twig bundle.

Materials & Tools

storage box

reindeer moss

PVA glue (white household glue)

glue brush

small twigs

raffia

small cones

THE BEDROOM

Pressed flower lampshade

Whole pressed flower heads and petals have been used together to create the bold design for this lampshade, though a more subtle effect could be created using the petals alone. Pressed leaves would make an interesting alternative and could, perhaps, be used around the rim of the shade. Pressing flowers or leaves is a simple process (see page 19) and you don't need a flower press to do it – a heavy book will be just as good.

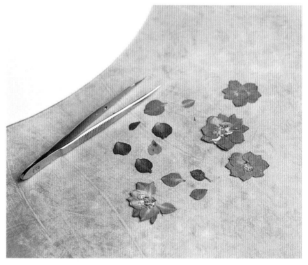

1. First select the flowers to decorate the lampshade. Pick out those with the best shapes and reserve them to use as whole flowers. Separate the remaining flowers into individual petals by gently pulling apart with tweezers.

2. Thin some glue with a little water. Hold one of the whole flowers gently with the tweezers and apply spots of glue to the back using a wooden skewer. Position the flower on the shade and press gently into place. Repeat with the other flowers.

Materials & Tools

plain lampshade

pressed flowers

PVA glue

wooden skewer

tweezers

glue brush

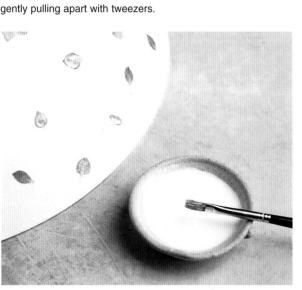

3. Fill the spaces between the flowers with individual petals, adding more until you are happy with the design. When the glue is dry, thin some more glue down to a runny consistency and paint each flower and petal with it to seal and protect.

Lavender bags

These little drawstring lavender bags can be used in a variety of ways. They could be hung in a wardrobe, placed in a linen cupboard or tucked between pillows on the bed. The fragrance of lavender not only has a pleasant, calming effect, but it also has the advantage of deterring moths. Should the lavender lose its fragrance, a few drops of lavender oil will help to rejuvenate it.

Materials & Tools

gingham, 30x23cm (12x9in)

plain fabric, 30x15cm (12x6in)

fabric offcut for motif

needle and cotton

dressmaking pins, scissors

cotton tape, wooden beads

dried lavender flowers

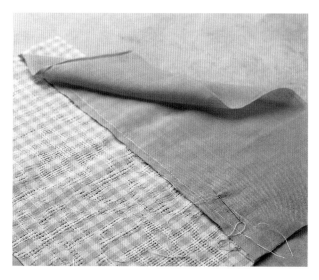

1. Lay the gingham face down and fold over one long edge by 5cm (2in). Lay the plain fabric on top, face down, with the bottom edge aligned with the raw edge of gingham. Sew one seam just in from the edge and another 1cm (1/2in) above it.

2. Leave a seam allowance at both ends of the seams. Now fold the gingham and plain fabric top in half, right sides together. Sew along the bottom and up the open side, leaving the space between the two previous seams free. Leave the top open.

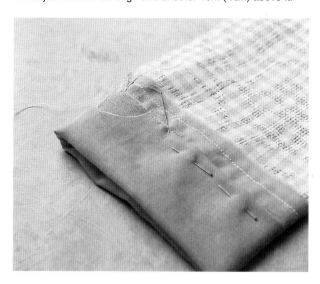

3. Fold over the top of the plain fabric by 2.5cm (1in) then roll over again, bringing the folded edge down to just above the top row of stitching. Pin and then slip stitch in place, leaving the bag opening free. Next thread the cotton tape through the casing.

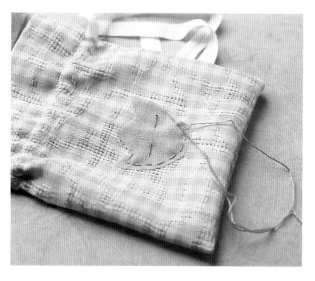

4. Turn the bag through to the right side and bring the tape ends through the gap in the side seam. Tie the beads to the ends. Cut a tulip shape from the fabric offcut. Pin and sew to the bag with running stitch. Fill the bag with lavender and tie closed.

Pot pourri candle

Materials & Tools

candle wax

rectangular moulds

pot pourri with rose buds

candle wick

scissors

wax boil bags or saucepan and

heat-proof bowl

Dried petals and rosebuds caught in the wax make a very pretty and aromatic candle to cheer up a corner of the bedroom. Making candles at home is not as hard as it may seem. All it needs is careful handling when melting and pouring molten wax and there are products designed to make this easier. For example, special boil bags are easy to handle and keep the wax contained, leaving no mess to clean up.

1. Melt the candle wax following the instructions on the packet, either in a boil bag or in a bowl over a saucepan of hot water. Pour into the four rectangular moulds and leave for two minutes. These four rectangles will form the candle sides.

2. After two minutes, scatter pot pourri over the wax and place in the refrigerator for an hour to harden. If you do not have moulds, pour the wax into a shallow dish or tin, add the pot pourri as here, then cut into rectangles before it hardens fully.

3. Pour a little molten wax into the bottom of one of the moulds. Before it sets, stand the four side pieces into it making sure the corners meet and the sides are standing straight.

4. Once the wax at the base has set, pour molten wax into the centre to fill the candle, positioning the wick as you go. Fill the candle almost to the top of the sides and leave the wax to harden. Never leave a burning candle unattended.

Rose and peony baskets

These pretty baskets are easy to make and are a lovely addition to any bedroom. They are filled with a selection of dried flowers, including roses, peonies and purple achillea. The peonies are particularly pretty and look like they are made from tissue paper. These ones have been reduced in size by removing the outer petals. All these flowers can be dried at home, using silica gel crystals for best results.

1. Separate out the dried flowers and select some for the basket. Cut their stems down to about 4cm (1¹/₂in) long. If you are using dried peonies, remove some of their outer petals if the heads are too large for the scale of the basket.

2. Cut the foam down to the shape of the basket to fit snugly inside. If you need two pieces to make the shape, glue them together. Pin moss around the edges of the foam, overlapping onto the top of the heart. Place the foam in the basket.

Materials & Tools

heart-shaped basket

dry florist's foam

glue

knife

dried sheet moss

wire pins

dried flowers

tweezers

scissors

3. Work around the edge of the basket, inserting flowers into the foam at an outward-facing angle. Use tweezers to insert the flowers close together, then fill the centre of the heart with the flowers upright. Position the flowers in groups for best effect.

Lavender wreath

Materials & Tools

dried lavender

reel wire, florist's stub wires

brown gutta percha tape

long, dry, pliable stems, such

as clematis

string, gingham ribbon

strong scissors

This wreath is simple to make using pliable stems such as clematis to make the base, then adding small bunches of lavender to decorate. While shaping the base, you will find that stray ends of stem come free. Trim off the longer pieces to give the heart shape definition, but leave the smaller ones to add to the rustic feel. Dried mimosa, with its distinctive fragrance and yellow colour, could be used instead.

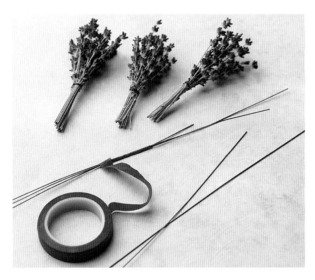

1. Make up bunches of lavender, wire the stems together and trim down. Take three stub wires and bind together with gutta percha, staggering the ends. As you reach the end of each wire, add another and carry on until it is long enough to make a heart.

2. When you have bent the tape-covered wires into a heart, take a handful of stems and bend around the wire base. Use reel wire to attach them to the heart at its top point, then bring the stems down to the point, cross them over and wire to the heart again.

3. Starting at the top of the heart, tie the bunches of lavender to the wreath using string. Face all the heads in the same direction and work down to the bottom of the heart, spacing them evenly. Repeat down the other side.

4. Make a hanging loop with string, attaching it to the wire at the top centre of the heart. Tie some string around the bottom of the heart to hide the wire there, then add a gingham ribbon to finish.

Scented muslin sachets

Because muslin is loosely woven, it allows fragrances to permeate through it, making it the perfect fabric for these scented drawer sachets. They are not only good for scenting drawers and linen chests, but add a thoughtful touch when left on the pillow when guests come to stay. The pot pourri is enclosed in a separate bag inside the sachet. This bag can be discarded and replaced when the fragrance fades.

Materials & Tools

paper envelope

stiff muslin

pot pourri

needle and cotton, pins

embroidery thread, scissors

button

thin ribbon

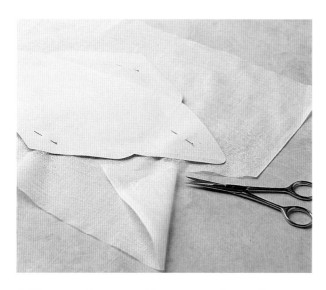

1. Steam open the seams of the paper envelope and use as a template. Pin it on the muslin and cut around it, leaving an extra 1cm (1/2in) as a seam allowance. Also cut a rectangle of muslin, fold in half and sew up three sides to make a pocket.

2. Turn the pocket through to enclose the seams, fill with lavender and sew the last side shut. Take the envelope piece and turn over a seam on all sides. Pin in place, enclosing the raw edges. Slip stitch the seams and remove the pins.

3. Bring three corners of the envelope together and pin to hold in place. Using three strands of embroidery thread together, cross stitch the two diagonal seams, making sure you do not pass the needle through the front of the envelope.

4. Sew the button in place where the two seams meet and use the thin ribbon to make a loop on the tip of the top point. This will act as a button hole. Finally, place the pocket of pot pourri in the envelope and pass the button through the loop to secure.

THE BATHROOM

Seaside mirror

All you need to make this handsome mirror is a plain frame and a variety of items from the seashore. You could use just shells, or include pebbles, dried seaweed, driftwood and starfish too. A glue gun will be a great help with this project: as the glue dries so quickly, you can build up the collage without displacing other items. You can also hold the mirror up and view it from the correct angle as you work.

1. Use the glue gun to stick pieces of reindeer moss and oak moss to the frame. Aim to achieve an even covering, mixing patches of the two.

2. Position the larger items first such as the big shells. You could either make a balanced arrangement of shells on all sides of the frame or position more at the bottom.

3. Fill the spaces between the large shells with small shells and finish with a few feature items such as starfish. Check all the items are glued firmly in place and remove any strands of glue.

Materials & Tools

mirror with a plain frame

reindeer moss

dried oak moss

selection of shells

starfish

glue gun

Mosaic shell box

Small shells can be very delicate and pretty and here they have transformed plain balsa wood boxes into attractive storage boxes which would complement any bathroom setting. You could make the design as simple or intricate as you like, but always arrange the shells on a flat surface first so you can adjust the design before gluing the shells to the box. Wash and dry the shells and gravel before you start.

1. Arrange the clean, dry shells on a flat surface before you begin and adjust the design as necessary until you are happy with the result.

2. Use strong adhesive and a fine brush to stick the shells to the side of the box. Position the central shell first, then stick the others around it. Allow the glue to dry.

Materials & Tools

balsa wood box

small shells

strong glue

glue brush

alpine gravel

3. Finish by sticking the gravel around the rim of the box. Apply glue to the area you want the gravel, then press the gravel onto the glue with your hand. Allow to dry then shake off the excess.

Herbal bath sachets

Materials & Tools

2 pieces of sheer cotton fabric,
25x45cm (10x18in)

20cm (8in) of cotton tape

small shells and glue

needle and cotton, scissors

white muslin circles, wool

herbal bath mixture

There is nothing more relaxing at the end of a hard day than a long, hot bath. These herbal bath sachets will make it even more relaxing and soothing, and look pretty too. Fill with this basic mixture, adapting as you wish: 1 cup of oatmeal, $1/2$ cup of powdered milk and $1/4$ cup each of wheat bran, dried lavender, dried soapwort flowers and leaves, and dried rose petals. Discard the inner sachets after use.

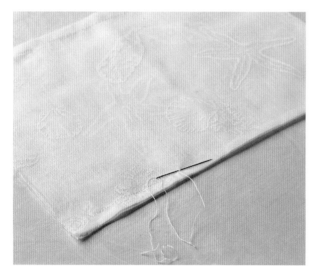

1. Place the two pieces of fabric wrong sides together and sew a seam around three sides, leaving a short side open. Trim the seams and turn inside out. Press, then sew a second seam around the bag for added strength, enclosing the raw edges.

2. Turn the top of the bag down by 4cm (1$1/2$in), turn under the raw edge and sew in place around the bag. Turn the bag through the right way, then press.

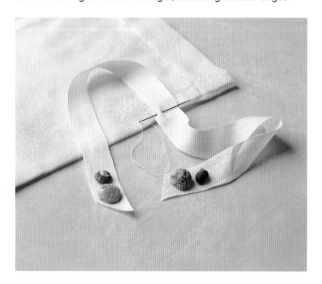

3. Cut the ends of the cotton tape at an angle and stick two small shells to each end. Sew the centre of the tape to one seam of the bag, making sure it is firmly fixed.

4. Place about two teaspoons of bath mixture in the centre of each circle of muslin, draw up all the edges and tie into a small parcel with a piece of wool. Place a sachet into the bag and drop under the hot tap.

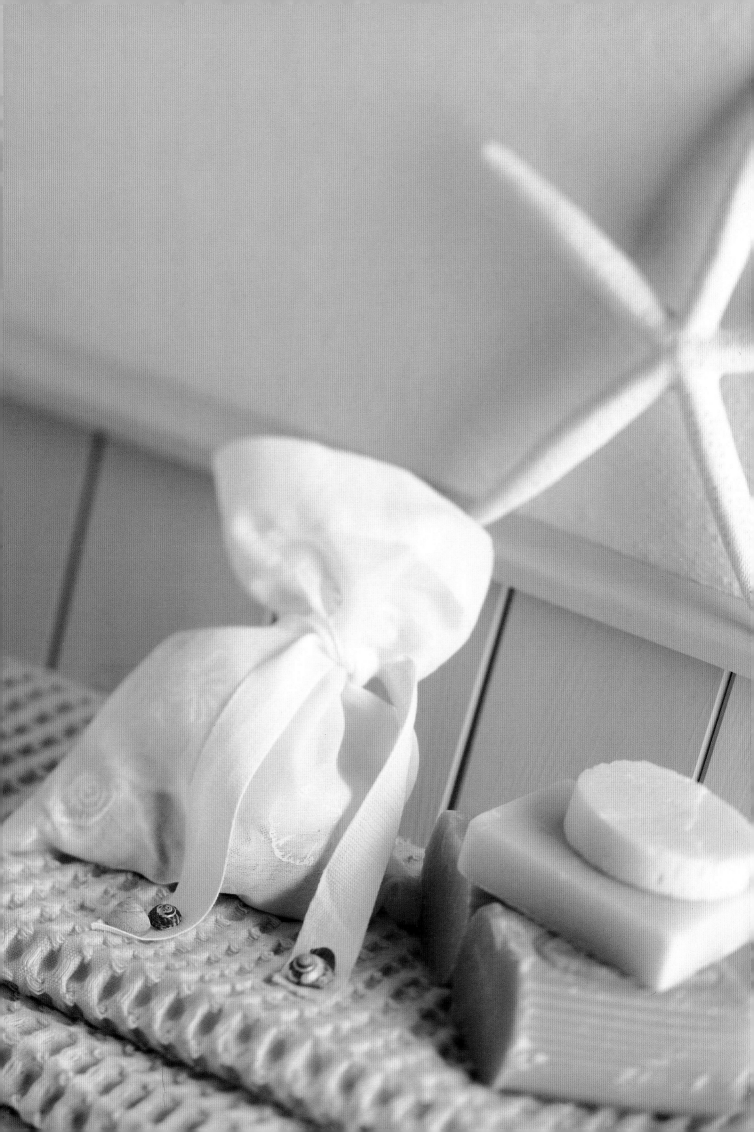

Pebble shelf

There is always a need for extra shelf space in a bathroom for all those bottles and containers that seem to accumulate there. But shelving can be decorative as well as functional. This basic unit has a pretty shape which has been enhanced with small pebbles and gravel, though shells would do just as well. If you can't get a unit with a decorative edge, you could still use the same idea on a plain shelf.

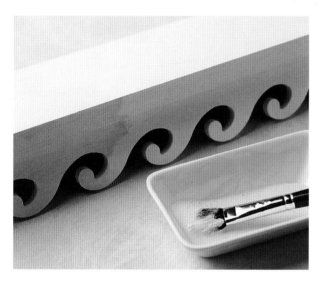

1. Prepare and paint the shelf as necessary to achieve a smooth, white base coat. Take a small amount of pale beige glaze onto the brush and lightly colour the shelf, creating a light, dragged effect.

2. When the glaze is dry, glue individual pieces of gravel along the edge of the shelf, following the shape of the decorative edge if your shelf has one. Allow the glue to dry then check all the pieces are held firmly in position.

Materials & Tools

plain shelf

white acrylic paint

pale beige acrylic glaze

small paint brush

washed gravel

pebbles

strong glue

glue brush

3. Next glue a line of pebbles along the top edge of the shelf, mixing colours and sizes as you go. Arrange them at different angles to create a random effect.

Coat pegs

Materials & Tools

coat peg rack, shells

tile adhesive/grouting

white acrylic primer

blue and green acrylic glazes

mid blue acrylic paint

soft cloth, paint brush

sandpaper, matt varnish

The shells that decorate this coat peg rack have been fixed on with tile adhesive. This fills the gap between the wood and the shell, giving the appearance that the shell is an integral part of the rack. You can use any shells you like, but make sure they have an edge that will lie flat against the rack. Here we have used both green and blue glazes to add extra depth of colour to the peg rack: choose any two colours you like.

1. Generously fill the back of each shell with tile adhesive and press it firmly onto the wood. Allow the excess adhesive to squeeze out around the shell then remove it with a damp finger. Fix a shell in each of the gaps between the pegs.

2. When the tile adhesive is dry, give the whole thing, including the shells, two coats of primer and allow to dry. Next use a soft cloth to apply a coat of blue glaze. Work the glaze into a soft, blotchy layer, filling pockets and cracks as you go.

3. When the blue glaze is completely dry, repeat the process with the green glaze. Use the cloth to work the glaze until you are happy with the effect. Glazes take longer to dry than paints, so you will have time to achieve exactly the right finish.

4. Paint a small motif under each of the pegs using the blue acrylic paint. Once dry, sand all over the surface lightly with the sandpaper to give a distressed finish, concentrating on certain points to give a more natural effect. Finish with a coat of varnish.

Rope and shell beakers

These plain plastic beakers have been transformed by the addition of natural rope and a few shells. You could decorate any container in this way, though it is probably inadvisable to use clear plastic or glass as you will be able to see the glue through it. Decorate a variety of containers of different sizes and use them to store bathroom clutter such as toothbrushes, toothpaste, combs and razors.

1. First glue the end of the rope to the side of the beaker at the bottom. Allow the glue to dry to prevent the rope slipping as you proceed. Next run a line of glue in a spiral round the sides of the beaker to the top, sticking the rope in position as you go.

Materials & Tools

beaker

rope or cord

glue

glue brush

scissors

shells

2. When you reach the top of the beaker, continue the cord in a ring around the rim. Cut the end where it meets the start of the ring of rope and glue the end firmly in position. Cover the end with a good coating of glue to prevent the strands unravelling.

3. Stick the first shell over the top end of the rope to cover it, then add more shells in a random fashion over the beaker. You may need to allow the glue on the first few to dry before you add the others to prevent dislodging them as you work.

THE GARDEN

Seashell pots

This is a simple but effective idea with endless variation: use your imagination to create any number of different patterns. Here we have restricted the decoration to the rim of the pot, but you could decorate the sides too, perhaps substituting the reindeer moss for a number of other shells and arranging them mosaic-fashion on the side of the pot. These flower pots could also be used as candle holders outside.

1. Select a number of shells of a similar size and glue them in a neat row around the edge of the pot. Use a strong adhesive that dries clear. Allow the glue to dry.

2. Cut some reindeer moss into small pieces and stick them around and between the shells to cover the rim of the pot. Make sure the moss does not hide the shells.

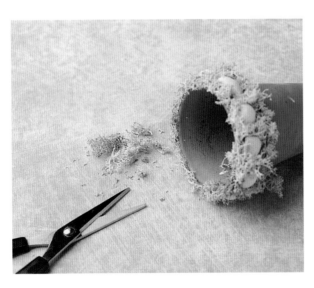

3. When the glue is dry, trim away the excess moss with scissors to leave a neat edge around the rim of the pot. You can also trim away any pieces of moss covering the shells.

Materials & Tools

terracotta pots

shells

reindeer moss

scissors

glue and glue brush

Twig trellis

Making a small trellis panel from twigs is quite straightforward and the finished product benefits from a rough, rustic finish. Obviously you can make the trellis panel any size you like, just select a number of twigs or small branches of the right size and as straight as possible. If you plan to attach the trellis to a wall, remember to leave a gap between it and the wall to give the plant space to grow.

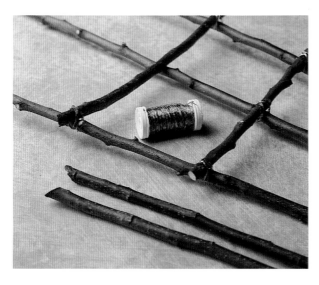

1. Cut three pieces of twig to an equal length for the uprights. Cut four for the cross pieces of varying sizes: the largest for the uppermost cross piece and the smallest for the lower one. Lay them in position and bind the joints together with reel wire.

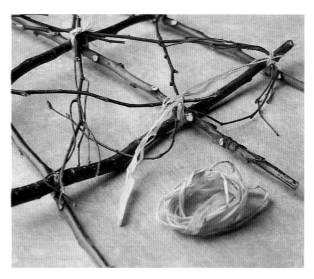

2. When the basic structure is wired tightly together, add some fine twigs to form crosses in the square holes. Tie the twigs to the framework with raffia, which will also serve to cover the wire.

Materials & Tools

thick, straight twigs

thinner twigs for infill

reel wire

raffia

strong scissors or pruning

shears

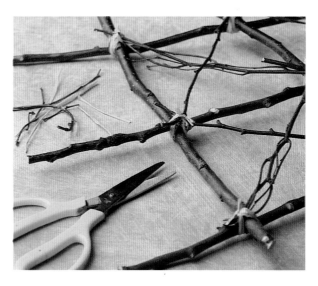

3. Trim the raffia ends as short as possible and neaten the ends of the twigs using strong scissors or pruning shears. Lastly, cut the bottom ends of the three uprights to a point so they will be easier to push into the soil.

Leaf printed chair

It is surprisingly easy to create a stamp using a soft sponge and a leaf. The leaves you choose should be as fresh as possible with prominent veins to create a strong pattern. Be careful when applying paint to the leaf stamp, and avoid pools of paint which will distort the pattern. It is a good idea to practise on a scrap of paper before you begin so that you can avoid costly mistakes.

1. Paint the top of the large leaf with glue and press onto the sponge. Once dry, cut around the leaf shape, trimming the sponge as necessary. Repeat with the small leaf. Next, cut two rectangles of sponge, each slightly larger than one of the leaves.

2. Brush red paint onto the surface of the large rectangular sponge, aiming for an even distribution. Lay the canvas on a flat surface and press the sponge onto it to create the pattern, adding more paint as necessary. Repeat with the smaller one.

Materials & Tools

canvas garden chair

leaves with prominent veins

glue

kitchen sponges

scissors

red fabric paint

green fabric paint

paint brush

3. When the paint is dry, apply green paint to the leaves and make a leaf print over each rectangle, the small leaves on the small rectangles and the large on the large. Leave to dry, then iron to set the paint, following the manufacturer's instructions.

Moss topiary

This is a quick way to create architectural shapes that will imitate the real living topiary that can be seen in grand gardens. These moss shapes are purely decorative and can be used on their own or added to a collection of plants and flowers to give structure to the display. They can be made to any size or shape you like and, unlike true topiary, won't need constant trimming and watering.

1. Press the cane into the centre of the foam in the topiary base and glue around the top edge to hold in place. Glue the topiary base into the terracotta flower pot. A glue gun will be a help with this project as the glue it dispenses dries very quickly.

Materials & Tools

terracotta pot

foam topiary base

dry florist's foam ball

15cm (6in) cane

dried sheet moss

wire staples

scissors

glue and glue brush

2. Cover the top of the cane with glue and press the foam ball onto it until the ball sits on the rim of the pot. Pin pieces of sheet moss onto the surface of the ball to cover, using wire staples. Push the pins right into the foam so they are hidden by the moss.

3. Continue adding moss until the ball is totally covered, making sure the pieces are butted up tightly together. Trim off any straggly moss ends, but take care that you do not expose the foam in the process.

123

Twig candle holder

It is always pleasant to dine outside on warm summer evenings and a candle on the table adds to the ambience. This handsome candle holder has been made from a tiny galvanized bucket decorated with small twigs and leaves. It is not difficult to make candles; the only tricky part is keeping the wick in position while you pour the wax around it. Here we have used chopsticks to hold the wick steady.

1. Place two elastic bands together around the middle of the bucket. Cut all the twigs to the height of the bucket and slide them under the elastic bands, working your way around the bucket and arranging the twigs close together.

2. Select a number of leaves of the same size and glue them around the elastic bands to hide them. Overlap the leaves to create a wreath effect.

3. Melt the wax in a boil bag or a bowl over a saucepan of hot water. Pour a little wax into the bucket and set the wick in place, holding it upright while the wax sets. Top up with more wax, almost to the rim, still supporting the wick until the wax sets.

Materials & Tools

small galvanized bucket

straight twigs

2 elastic bands

preserved or fresh leaves

glue and glue brush

candle wax

candle wick

boil bags for wax (optional)

chopsticks or something similar

pruning shears

Pressed leaf candle

Candles are available in numerous colours and textures and many are very attractive, particularly the handmade varieties with a mottled finish which has here been enhanced by the addition of some leaves. The leaves have been pressed to make sure they lie flat on the candle sides and are held in place with wax which is painted onto the leaf backs when molten and sets to stick them in position.

1. Press the leaves following the instructions on page 19. When they are ready, select a number of a similar size and shape to use around the base of the candle, handling them with tweezers to prevent damage.

2. Melt a little wax in either a boil bag or a bowl over a saucepan of hot water. Working quickly, brush the leaf backs with wax and press into position on the candle. If the wax hardens on the brush, dip in hot water to melt it again.

Materials & Tools

candle

leaves

flower press or heavy book

wax

boil bag for wax (optional)

small paint brush

raffia

3. Once all the leaves are in position and you are happy with the design, tie a length of raffia around the leaves to decorate.

127

Index